HEROES

Contents

Wilma Rudolph

Written by Kerrie Ann Capobianco
Illustrated by Marjorie Scott

1940

Wilma Rudolph
was born with polio.
Polio made Wilma's legs weak.
It was hard for Wilma
to use her left leg.
It was hard for Wilma to walk.

Wilma's mother
took her to the doctor.
The doctor said,
"Rub the leg every day!"
Wilma's mother and brothers
and sisters rubbed her leg
four times a day.
The rubbing helped
Wilma's leg.

1945

When Wilma was five,
the doctor put a brace
on her leg.
The brace helped Wilma walk.
Wilma had to wear the brace
all the time.

1951

One day, Wilma took the brace off her leg.
She went to church without the brace.
She could walk without the brace.

1954

Wilma liked to play sports.
She liked to play basketball.

Wilma liked to run.
She liked to run in races.
She went to track meets.
At her first track meet,
Wilma lost all the races.
Wilma needed a coach to help her.
A man named Ed Temple
was a good coach.
He coached Wilma.
Wilma trained hard.

1958

Wilma went to
Tennessee State University.
She worked hard.
She trained hard.
She ran races.
She did part-time work
so she could stay
in school.

What kind of things do coaches do to help athletes?

1960

Wilma went
to the Olympic Games
in Rome.
She ran in
the 100-meter race.
She ran in
the 200-meter race.
And she ran in
the 400-meter relay race.
Wilma won
all her races.
She won
three gold medals.
She was the first
American woman
to win three gold medals.

Daily Reporter

November 1994

Wilma Rudolph died today.

She did what people said was too hard. She beat the polio that she had. She walked. She ran. She raced. She won! Wilma Rudolph was a hero.

Bubbles

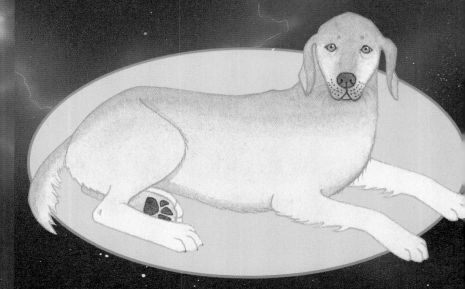

Written by Janet Slater Bottin
Illustrated by Phyllis Pollema-Cahill

Bubbles woke up.
She could hear strange sounds.
She looked up at the bed.
Melissa was asleep.
Bubbles looked after Melissa.
Bubbles helped Melissa hear things.

Melissa could not hear sounds.
She could not hear low sounds.
She could not hear high sounds.
She could not hear the strange sounds
that Bubbles could hear.
Bubbles lay down again.
She put her head on her paws.

Then she heard the strange sound again!
It was a bad sound!
The sound came from
the twins' bedroom!
Bubbles didn't bark.
Melissa would not hear her
if she barked.
Bubbles jumped up onto Melissa's bed.
Then she jumped down
onto the floor again.
Up… down… up… down… up… down.

What are some strange sounds that you might hear in the night?

Melissa woke up. She sat up.
"What do you want, Bubbles?
Do you want to go out?"
she said.

Melissa got out of bed.
She went to the door.
Bubbles ran
to the twins' bedroom!
Melissa said,
"What is it, Bubbles?"
Bubbles jumped
at the door
of the twins'
bedroom.

What do you think
Bubbles has heard?

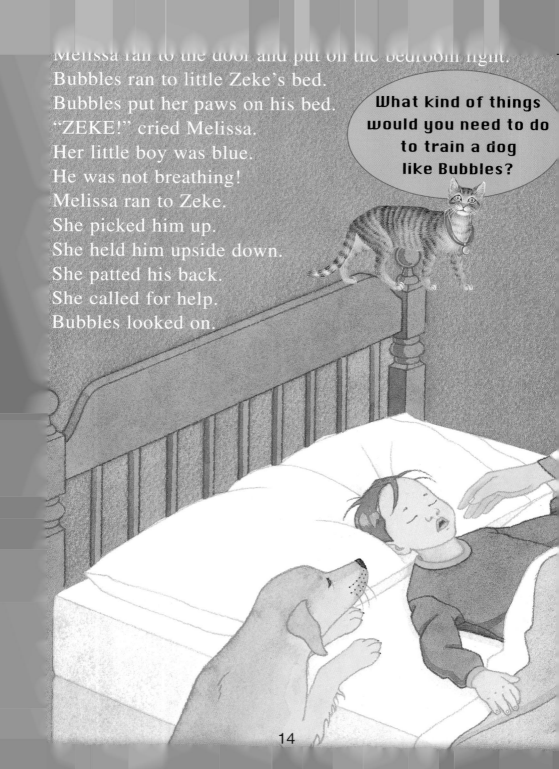

Melissa ran to the door and put off the bedroom light.
Bubbles ran to little Zeke's bed.
Bubbles put her paws on his bed.
"ZEKE!" cried Melissa.
Her little boy was blue.
He was not breathing!
Melissa ran to Zeke.
She picked him up.
She held him upside down.
She patted his back.
She called for help.
Bubbles looked on.

What kind of things would you need to do to train a dog like Bubbles?

14

Bubbles heard the ambulance.
She saw people come to help.
She saw Melissa and little Zeke
get into the ambulance.
She heard the ambulance drive away.

She had helped her friend Melissa.
She had saved little Zeke.

Daily Reporter

Hearing Dog, Bubbles, a Hero

Bubbles, a ten-year-old hearing dog, saved a child today. Bubbles woke up her owner, Melissa, when she heard a strange sound. Zeke, one of Melissa's twins, had stopped breathing.

This is not the first time that Bubbles has helped Melissa. One time, Bubbles saved Melissa when a log fell out of the fire.

Another time, Bubbles saved Melissa when she had a crash in her car.

Bubbles is a real hero!

Brent Meldrum

Written by
Sharon Capobianco
Illustrated by Jeannie Ferguson

From a true story:

Brent Meldrum and his friend
Tanya Branden were playing.
Tanya was eating something.
All of a sudden, Tanya began to choke.
Something was stuck
in her throat.
Tanya could not breathe.
She went blue.

Brent knew that
he had to help Tanya.
He had to stop
his friend from choking,
or she might die.
He had seen a person
choking on television.
He had seen what people did
to save the person's life.
He was going to do that
for Tanya.

Always be careful
eating things that
could stick in your
throat!

Brent went behind Tanya.
He put his arms around her.
He put his hands together.
He pushed his thumbs up
under Tanya's ribs.
He lifted Tanya up,
off the ground.
Then he put her
back down again.
Tanya coughed up
what she was eating.
Brent had saved Tanya's life.

How do you think Brent felt about saving Tanya's life?

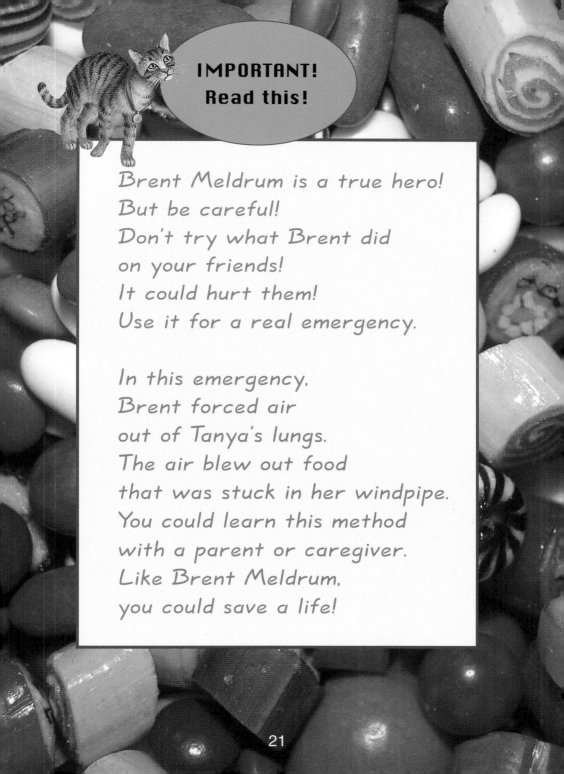

**IMPORTANT!
Read this!**

Brent Meldrum is a true hero!
But be careful!
Don't try what Brent did
on your friends!
It could hurt them!
Use it for a real emergency.

In this emergency,
Brent forced air
out of Tanya's lungs.
The air blew out food
that was stuck in her windpipe.
You could learn this method
with a parent or caregiver.
Like Brent Meldrum,
you could save a life!

A Five-year-old Hero

Today, a five-year-old boy saved the life of his friend. His friend Tanya was choking on something. Brent Meldrum used a method that helped his friend cough up what she was eating. A man named Henry Heimlich made up the method in 1974.

Reporter

Saves His Pal's Life

Heimlich showed people how to get out food that was stuck. Before he did this, lots of people had died from choking on food. We asked Brent to show us what he had done. Brent said he had seen the "Time-Life Remover" on TV. No matter what you call the method, it saved his pal's life.

Written by Louise Fenwick   Illustrated by Mrinal Mitra

Mother Cat was a street cat.
She was a very smart street cat.
Mother Cat had five little kittens.

At night, Mother Cat went out to find food.
"I will be back soon," she said to her kittens.

One night, Mother Cat
got the food and set out for home.
When she got near her home,
Mother Cat heard a strange sound.
She saw tall flames jump up into the sky.
Her home was on fire!

What are some things that street cats have to learn about?

25

Mother Cat ran into her home.
She ran into the flames.
She ran to the place
where her little kittens were.
"I will get you out,"
she said to her kittens.

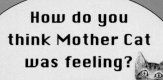

Mother Cat got the first little kitten
by the back of the neck.
She ran into the flames and out on to the street.
"Stay here," she said.
"I will come back with your brothers and sisters."

Mother Cat went back into the flames.
She took the second little kitten out.

Then she took the third little kitten out.

And then she took the fourth little kitten
out from the fire and on to the street.

Then she ran back into her home
for the last time.

The fifth little kitten lay still.
Its fur was hot.

"Oh no!" cried Mother Cat.
She picked up the little kitten.
She ran into the flames and out on to the street.

She put the little kitten down by her other kittens.
She began to lick its hot fur.

A firefighter came over.
He sat down by Mother Cat.
He looked at the kittens, one by one.

"It's all right," he said to Mother Cat.
"All your kittens are safe."
The firefighter put Mother Cat and her kittens in a box.
He took them to the vet.

"You are a very brave cat," said the vet.
She washed Mother Cat's fur.
She rubbed some cream on Mother Cat's burns.

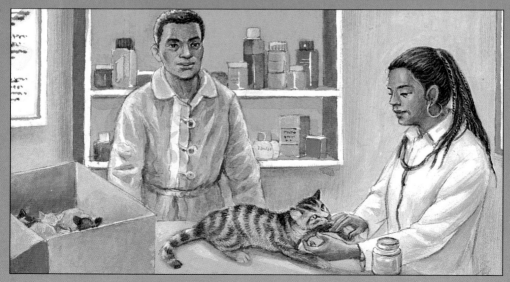

The firefighter took Mother Cat
and her five little kittens to live with him.
He called the kittens
Sooty, Cinders, Flame, Firefly, and Smokey.
Mother Cat did not have to go out at night
to find food again.

What event changed Mother Cat's life?

31

Books in the **WILDCATS™** Series

	People and Places	Science and Technology	Sport and Action	Myths and Misconceptions
WILDCATS Lion	Purple Walrus and Other Perfect Pets / HEROES	Photos, Photos	STREET ACTION / Fire! Fire!	What Do You Think? / Dragons Galore
WILDCATS Tiger	Long Ago and Far Away / Incredible Places	Eruption / Maps and Codes	RESCUE! / Woods Lions and Greens	Dinosaur Detective / Hercules and other Greek Legends
WILDCATS Bobcat	TWISTERS and Other Wind Storms / The Four A's	Eye Spy / UP IN THE AIR	Special Effects / Appointment with Action	Another Point of View / RIGHT or WRONG?
WILDCATS Leopard	Rain Forest / The Sky's the Limit	Spreading the Word	Surf's Up / Extreme Sports	NOT WHAT IT SEEMS / Mythical Beasts